Reclaiming the Cross

Reclaiming the Cross

A STUDY OF THE MEANINGS OF THE CRUCIFIXION

DARREN CUSHMAN WOOD

North United Methodist Church • Indianapolis, IN

© 2023 North United Methodist Church, 3808 N. Meridian St., Indianapolis, IN 46208. NorthChurchIndy.com.

ISBN 979-8-9882332-1-3 (epub)

ISBN 979-8-9882332-2-0 (paperback)

The cover art comes from a small portion of one of the many beautiful banners throughout North United Methodist Church created by the late Doris Douglas, a long-time member, and other artists.

Biblical quotations from the New Revised Standard Version of the Bible, copyright © 1989 by the Division of Christian Education of the National Council of the Churches of Christ in the USA and used by permission.

Hymn quotations from The United Methodist Hymnal, copyright © 1989 by the United Methodist Publishing House and from The Faith We Sing, copyright © 2000 by Abingdon Press and used by permission.

Contents

Introduction   1

Part I. Main Body

1. A Victorious Defeat: The Cross as Victory   7

2. A Graceful Solidarity: The Cross as Solidarity   13

3. An Unexpected Peace: The Cross as Reconciliation   19

4. A Dying Life: The Cross as Participation   27

5. A Necessary Obedience: The Cross as Obedience   35

About the Author   41

Introduction

Hanging from the center of the ceiling in McCleary Chapel at the University of Indianapolis is a Jerusalem cross — a cross with four equal sides and four smaller crosses filling in the four quadrants above and beneath the arms of the cross. Normally a communion table is placed directly below it, but when the table is removed the cross hangs low enough to nearly hit your head. Everything else in the room is movable but the cross. No matter where you sit you can see it, and no matter what the arrangement or decorations may be, the cross is in the middle of it all.

THE UNAVOIDABLE CROSS

So it is in our Christian faith. Adore it or abhor it, the cross hangs in the middle of the Christian religion. You simply cannot have Christianity without the cross lest you abandon the core narrative of the New Testament. Indeed, Paul summarized his message by saying, "We preach Christ crucified." (1 Corinthians 1:23)

Yet there is no other symbol in Christianity that has had as contentious a history as the cross. It has been used by Crusaders as a sign of conquest and as an example of servitude by slave masters and abusive husbands. To the other extreme, the cross was an inspiration for nonviolent protests in the civil rights movement. The cross is a potent symbol precisely because it is a multivalent symbol capable of great good and great evil depending on how it is understood.

CROSSES AND BASEBALL DIAMONDS

This gives us all the more reason to meditate on the cross in order to discover its true meaning. Rather, I should say "meanings" because there is more than one way to think about the cross.

Despite its centrality, Christian tradition never said there is only one correct interpretation. For example, the Apostles' and Nicene Creeds affirm that Jesus "suffered under Pontius Pilate, was crucified, dead and buried," but they do not explain *how* the cross works as part of our salvation. And so, over the years there have been a variety of "atonement theories," and each one has been accepted as part of basic Christian beliefs.

As with other doctrines, there is a wideness within orthodoxy that allows for diverse opinions about the cross while at the same time recognizing that there are limits to what is an acceptable interpretation or application of the cross.

Think of doctrine like a baseball diamond. In baseball there are foul lines that fan out from home plate. Balls hit outside those lines are foul, but a variety of balls can be hit within those lines that are fair.

When it comes to the cross, we believe that the cross is an essential part of the story of salvation. But when it comes to the details about its role — how the cross works — there are a variety of valid perspectives.

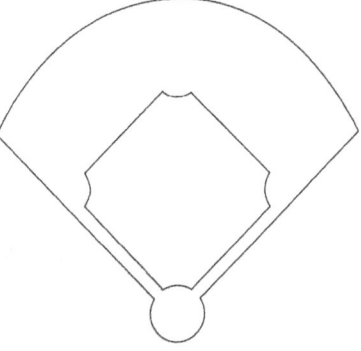

The diversity of perspectives comes, in part, from different assumptions we make about other things that shape how we see the cross.

One of those assumptions is how we see the problem of sin and evil. If the cross is the "solution" (or part of the solution), then you have to ask, "What is the problem it is supposed to solve?" How you define the nature of sin shapes how you describe the cross.

Another assumption that shapes how we see the cross is the role of other beliefs, especially the incarnation and the resurrection. The relationship between the crucifixion and these beliefs puts the spin on our view of the cross. The introductions to each session explains these underlying assumptions.

THIS STUDY

This study is designed for individual reflection or small group discussion. Each session includes questions to get you started and to take you deeper into the weekly topic that is highlighted by one or two key scripture passages. Because the cross is a contested symbol, you are encouraged to explore your options and articulate your criticisms of the various ways in which that symbol has been misused.

Concluding each session is a section called "What We Believe" and "What We Reject" that clarifies the boundaries and diversity of orthodox belief. This is the baseball diamond of belief. It is included to help you clarify where you stand in relationship to church doctrine, regardless of whether you decide to stand within or outside of it.

Ultimately the cross is more than an object of speculation. It is a symbol of faith. And so, each session ends with a meditation exercise that will help you discover the reality of the cross for today. The meditation exercises were created to appeal to different types of spirituality. Some are more rational and others are more imaginative; some involve action and others quiet reflection. If some of them do not speak to you, that is OK because there are a variety of ways to pray the cross.

You will notice that the key scripture passages are not the passion story from the four Gospels. Instead, they are passages that interpret the meaning of the cross. This is a study of the cross as a symbol of faith, not a study of the death of Jesus. Nevertheless, the story of Jesus' death is an inseparable part of understanding the meanings of the cross as a symbol.

It is my prayer that you will rediscover the meanings of the cross in ways that deepen your faith in Jesus Christ. Spiritual growth is often a painful process, especially when the cross is the focus of your exploration. Just as Jesus' crucifixion resulted in his resurrection, we claim the promise that "if we have been united with him in a death like his, we will certainly be united with him in a resurrection like his." (Romans 6:5)

Biblical quotations are from the New Revised Standard Version of the Bible, copyright © 1989 by the Division of

Christian Education of the National Council of the Churches of Christ in the USA and used by permission.

Hymn quotations are from The United Methodist Hymnal, copyright ©1989 by the United Methodist Publishing House and from The Faith We Sing, copyright ©2000 by Abingdon Press and used by permission.

Today, read Mark's passion story in Mark 14:43-15:47. Read it in one sitting.

Imagine yourself in the story. What do you see? What do you hear? What do you feel?

Spend several moments in silent prayer as you let the story set into your heart and mind.

Offer this prayer:

Spirit of God,
whose strange and saving wisdom
was revealed on the cross,
help us to die
to all preconceived notions
and pat answers,
so that we may be raised anew
into a greater knowledge
of your love and hope
in Jesus Christ the Word. Amen.

1. A Victorious Defeat: The Cross as Victory

GETTING STARTED

If you could design a sanctuary, where would you put a cross?

1. Up front and center, lifted above everything else;
2. Several crosses as part of the artwork and fixtures;
3. On a banner along with other banners that would change with the seasons;
4. At the entrance;
5. Carried in during the opening processional and taken out at the end, or
6. No cross.

INTRODUCTION

The early church turned the cross upside down. It was an instrument of imperial power. But because it is an essential part of the Jesus story, the early church could not ignore it. So instead, they reinterpreted it. Drawing upon the Passover story and the image of the suffering servant in Isaiah, they saw the cross as a sign of God's power to save us.

Crucifixion in the Roman Empire

According to John Dominic Crossan in "Jesus: A Revolutionary Biography," Roman crucifixion was state terrorism. It was a public form of torture that was often used with other forms, such as flogging. (In contrast, torture today is performed in secret. However, the purpose of torture, then and now, is not to get information from the victim. It is to inscribe on the individual the power of the State in order to maintain a climate of fear that enables the State to perpetuate its authority.)

It was a form of public humiliation and a deterrent to rebellion. Usually the victim was naked and hanging in a prominent place for all to see. Usually the body was not buried, but left as food for wild beasts and birds of prey. The death was supposed to be slow and painful.

Mass crucifixions were used to put down revolts. For example, after the death of Herod the Great in 4 b.c.e., Romans crucified 3,000 people after a massacre in the Temple during Passover. In the summer of A.D. 70, Titus's siege of Jerusalem included the crucifixion of 500 rebels in different positions for the amusement of the Roman troops.

The cross is the destruction of the very forces that killed Jesus, an ironic implosion of the evil that nailed him to the cross. Jesus' death is "the death of death." This view of the cross has been called "Christus Victor" — the victorious Christ.

If the cross is the solution, what then is the implied problem? The problem is domination. Sin and evil are in control, and we are being destroyed by these forces (whether they are spiritual, cultural, political, etc.). On the cross, God in Christ gives us victory over these forces.

Speaking about the African-American experience, Shawn Copeland wrote: "The cross was treasured because it enthroned the One who went all the way with them and for them. The enslaved Africans sang because they saw the results of the cross — triumph over the principalities and powers of death; triumph over evil in this world."[1]

The crucifixion is only one half of the solution. The resurrection is the other half that completes the victory.

The cross as victory entails a different way of looking at reality in the face of absurd and seemingly insurmountable suffering. God's power, as revealed in the cross and resurrection, operates very differently from the power dynamics in the world. The cross is part of a different logic; a different kind of wisdom. Thus, Paul describes Christ as "the power of God and the wisdom of God." (I Corinthians 1:24)

In this session, explore that ironic logic. The primary meaning of the cross is that it represents God's victory over sin, evil, and death. As you read and reflect, consider the alternative form of power the cross offers us and how easily the cross can be misused and misunderstood.

READING

1 Corinthians 1:18-25

[18]For the message about the cross is foolishness to those who are perishing, but to us who are being saved it is the power of God. [19]For it is written, "I will destroy the wisdom of the wise, and the discernment of the discerning I will thwart. [20]Where is the one who is wise? Where is the scribe? Where is the debater of this age? Has not God made foolish the wisdom of the world? [21]For since, in the wisdom of God, the world did not know God through wisdom, God decided, through the foolishness of our proclamation, to save those who believe. [22]For Jews demand signs and Greeks desire wisdom, [23]but we proclaim Christ crucified, a stumbling block to Jews and foolishness to Gentiles, [24]but to those who are the called, both Jews and Greeks, Christ the power of God and the wisdom of God. [25]For God's foolishness is wiser than human wisdom, and God's weakness is stronger than human strength.

REFLECTION QUESTIONS

What kinds of power do we see in the world today? How do they compare/contrast with the cross?

How does the cross give meaning and hope to those who are suffering?

How has the power of the symbol of the cross been misused?

What does it mean to you that Paul describes the cross as "the power and wisdom of God?"

If the cross is the power and wisdom of God, then how

should it shape our perspective on power dynamics (political, economic, cultural, familial, etc.) in the world today?

How does the church celebrate the victory of Christ? Is the cross a part of that celebration?

WHAT WE BELIEVE:

- The crucifixion and the resurrection are two inseparable parts of the story of salvation.
- The cross is the destruction of the forces of evil, sin, and death.
- The cross gives us a different way of understanding power dynamics in our world today.

WHAT WE REJECT:

- Death is a part of the way God intended the world to work.
- The cross is a symbol that endorses and perpetuates violence and oppression.

MEDITATION EXERCISE: 'IMAGINING VICTORY'

Step 1: Select an image of the cross (such as a painting, a wall hanging, or a yard display).

Step 2: Enter into a time of silence while focusing on the cross. Then read or sing the first stanza of "Lift High the Cross:"
[refrain] Lift high the cross,
the love of Christ proclaim

'till all the world adore his sacred name.

Come, Christians, follow this triumphant sign.
The hosts of God in unity combine. [refrain]

Step 3: Envision modern-day examples of evil, hatred, and injustice. (The examples may be on a large scale, such as international relations, or they may be on an intimate level, such as family dynamics.)

Step 4: Envision each one of those examples coming to an end and a new world of love and justice emerging. What does this new world look and sound like?

Step 5: Quiet your mind and focus on the cross again.

Step 6: Read or sing these stanzas of "Lift High the Cross:"
[refrain] Lift high the cross,
the love of Christ proclaim
'till all the world adore his sacred name.

Each newborn servant of the Crucified bears on the brow the seal of him who died. [refrain]

So shall our song of triumph ever be:
Praise to the Crucified for victory! [refrain]

2. A Graceful Solidarity: The Cross as Solidarity

GETTING STARTED

When you see a crucifix, what is your gut reaction?

1. Not much
2. Yuck
3. How sad
4. Looks Catholic
5. I'm inspired

INTRODUCTION

In "Trauma and Grace," Serene Jones describes her experiences with a self-defense class for survivors of domestic violence. The last session of the class coincided with her church's Maundy Thursday passion play. Four of the women attended the service with her. Afterwards, one of the women, Mari, spoke up: "This cross story, it's the only part of this Christian thing I like; I get it. And it's like He gets me. He knows."

Jones writes that Mari's words "capture well a long and complex thread of Christian interpretations of the cross that highlights the believer's experience of solidarity between themselves and Christ as the source of redemption."[2]

> ## Moral Influence Theory of Atonement
>
> The Apostles' and Nicene Creeds affirm that Jesus died on the cross, but they do not spell out how his death works to give us salvation. Throughout the centuries, theologians have tried to explain "how" Jesus's death saves us.
>
> One such "theory of atonement" is called "the moral influence" theory, which was first articulated by Peter Abelard in the early 12th century. The cross, according to this perspective, is the supreme expression of God's love. When we understand the cross, we are moved by this love to trust in God. This awakening to God's love is how the cross saves us.
>
> The strength of this theory is that it emphasizes love, instead of anger or punishment, as God's motivation.
>
> The weakness of the theory is the assumption that the image of the cross will elicit our loving response to God. It relies too much on human subjectivity to explain how the cross saves humanity.

In this session we will explore how the crucifixion is an expression of God's affinity with and sharing in the struggles of humanity. Jesus' experiences on the cross are the culmination of an entire life of solidarity with humanity. This solidarity is seen in the incarnation, which is the belief that Jesus is both fully human and fully God. The cross represents more than the death of a religious leader; it is a sign of God's participation in the human experience, or as Jürgen Moltmann calls it, "the Crucified God."[3]

For much of Christian history there was a tendency to deemphasize the human side of Christ, and this distorted the meaning of the cross. Various "atonement theories" about how the cross saves us portrayed the cross as an abstract theory. One result was that Christianity tended to ignore social injustice.

If God's solidarity is the solution, what is our problem?

We are alienated from God. Sin is separation or disconnection between humanity and God. To bridge that gap, God comes in the form of Jesus of Nazareth to retrace the whole human experience, including death.

This session explores why it is necessary to see the cross as God's act of suffering *with* humanity.

READINGS

Philippians 2:5-8

[5]Let the same mind be in you that was in Christ Jesus, [6] who, though he was in the form of God, did not regard equality with God as something to be exploited, [7] but emptied himself, taking the form of a slave, being born in human likeness. And being found in human form, [8] he humbled himself and became obedient to the point of death — even death on a cross

Isaiah 53:1-9

[1]Who has believed what we have heard? And to whom has the arm of the Lord been revealed? [2] For he grew up before him like a young plant, and like a root out of dry ground; he had no form or majesty that we should look at him, nothing in

his appearance that we should desire him.³ He was despised and rejected by others; a man of suffering and acquainted with infirmity; and as one from whom others hide their faces he was despised, and we held him of no account.⁴ Surely he has borne our infirmities and carried our diseases; yet we accounted him stricken, struck down by God, and afflicted. ⁵But he was wounded for our transgressions, crushed for our iniquities; upon him was the punishment that made us whole, and by his bruises we are healed. ⁶All we like sheep have gone astray; we have all turned to our own way, and the Lord has laid on him the iniquity of us all. ⁷He was oppressed, and he was afflicted, yet he did not open his mouth; like a lamb that is led to the slaughter, and like a sheep that before its shearers is silent, so he did not open his mouth. ⁸By a perversion of justice he was taken away. Who could have imagined his future? For he was cut off from the land of the living, stricken for the transgression of my people. ⁹They made his grave with the wicked and his tomb with the rich, although he had done no violence, and there was no deceit in his mouth.

REFLECTION QUESTIONS

Was there ever a time when you were hurting and the presence of a special person gave you comfort and hope?

When you have gone through hard times, has God felt close to you or absent from you?

How is the meaning of the cross distorted if we do not see it as part of the entire life and ministry of Jesus?

If Jesus is fully human and fully divine, what does his

suffering reveal about the nature of God? What does it reveal about God's relationship with humanity?

How is the cross an expression of God's love?

Isaiah 53 helped the first believers understand why Jesus died. Does Isaiah help or confuse us in understanding the cross today?

WHAT WE BELIEVE:

- The crucifixion is the culmination of the incarnation.
- Jesus' death is an expression of God's love for humanity.

WHAT WE REJECT:

- The symbol of the cross promotes and legitimates abuse.
- The symbol of the cross reinforces the shame of victims.

MEDITATION EXERCISE:
"THE WOUNDS OF CHRIST"

Meditations on the wounds of Christ is a tradition that dates back to the Middle Ages and has taken various forms. In this week's meditation exercise we adapt this ancient practice as a way to see the presence of Jesus among those who are suffering today.

Step 1: Center yourself in silence, opening your heart and mind to the leading of the Holy Spirit. With each wound, imagine Jesus in and among the people associated with the wound:

- Forehead of Christ — those who suffer from mental illness and addictions.
- Right hand of Christ — those who work with their hands in exploitative conditions.
- Left hand of Christ — those who are victims of abuse.
- Right foot of Christ—those who have been uprooted by wars and disasters.
- Left foot of Christ — those who are dominated by oppressive regimes, systems, and cultures.
- Side of Christ — the churches that are persecuted around the world.

Step 2: Once again, center yourself in silence. Recall a moment in your life when you were in pain, physically or emotionally. Visualize where you were at that time. Imagine Jesus being there with you, sharing your burden and comforting you.

Step 3: Read or sing "What Wondrous Love is This":
What wondrous love is this,
O my soul, O my soul,
what wondrous love is this, O my soul!
What wondrous love is this
that caused the Lord of life
to lay aside his crown for my soul, for my soul,
to lay aside his crown for my soul.

3. An Unexpected Peace: The Cross as Reconciliation

GETTING STARTED

Remember a time when you got in trouble as a child. What happened? How did you feel?

INTRODUCTION

Sometimes it takes a variety of metaphors to make a point. That is what Paul does in Romans 5 when he describes how the death of Jesus reconciles us with God. There is war and peace imagery ("we have peace with God" and "we were enemies"). In contrast to the Empire's geopolitical *pax*, the church declared that our true peace comes from Lord Jesus Christ and not the Caesar.

He also uses temple imagery. Just as the holy of holies is

where the priest meets God, the cross gives us "access to his grace."

Then there is a bit of legal imagery when he declares that we are "justified [acquitted; declared innocent] by his blood." Whether it is a battlefield, the holy of holies, or a courtroom, the message is the same: the cross reconciles us with God.

If the solution is reconciliation, what is the problem?

We are in a state of conflict with God. Sin is rebellion against God. We are at odds with God's will and fighting against God's ways.

Sometimes we confuse what is a normal part of how God made us with our sinful rebellion. We are created in the image of God, and salvation is the recovery of this image. But if we confuse this divine image with sin then our understanding of the cross is skewed.

The cross as God's act of reconciliation is based on additional assumptions. It assumes that Jesus's identity represents more than a lone individual. In some sense, he represents humanity to God and God to humanity.

The conflict with God spills over into our relationships with one another. The letter to the Ephesians describes how the cross also reconciles us with one another. This was a big problem in the early church between members who were Jewish.

Needless to say, the history of Christianity is as full of examples of our divisions as it is our unity. It raises the question "How can the cross be a symbol of reconciliation?"

In this session we explore the peace that Jesus's death creates with God, with others, and within us.

READINGS

Romans 5:1-2, 6-11

^{1}Therefore, since we are justified by faith, we have peace with God through our Lord Jesus Christ, ^{2}through whom we have obtained access to this grace in which we stand; and we boast in our hope of sharing the glory of God.

^{6}For while we were still weak, at the right time Christ died for the ungodly. ^{7}Indeed, rarely will anyone die for a righteous person — though perhaps for a good person someone might actually dare to die.
^{8}But God proves his love for us in that while we still were sinners Christ died for us. ^{9}Much more surely then, now that we have been justified by his blood, will we be saved through him from the wrath of God.
^{10}For if while we were enemies, we were reconciled to God through the death of his Son, much more surely, having been reconciled, will we be saved by his life. ^{11}But more than that, we even boast in God through our Lord Jesus Christ, through whom we have now received reconciliation.

Ephesians 2:11-17

^{11}So then, remember that at one time you Gentiles by birth, called 'the uncircumcision' by those who are called 'the circumcision' — a physical circumcision made in the flesh by human hands — ^{12}remember that you were at that time without Christ, being aliens from the commonwealth of Israel, and strangers to the covenants of promise, having no hope and without God in the world.
^{13}But now in Christ Jesus you who once were far off have

been brought near by the blood of Christ. ¹⁴For he is our peace; in his flesh he has made both groups into one and has broken down the dividing wall, that is, the hostility between us.

¹⁵He has abolished the law with its commandments and ordinances, so that he might create in himself one new humanity in place of the two, thus making peace, ¹⁶and might reconcile both groups to God in one body through the cross, thus putting to death that hostility through it. ¹⁷So he came and proclaimed peace to you who were far off, and peace to those who were near.

Substitutionary Theory of Atonement

The most familiar interpretation of "how" the cross saves us is the substitutionary theory of atonement.

According to this perspective, Christ was a substitute for us when he died on the cross, so that we would not have to face eternal punishment. It was first purposed by Anselm in the 11th century, who said that God's honor had been disgraced by human sin, and only the death of the God-Man Jesus could restore (satisfy) God's honor.

In the same vein, later theologians described the cross as Christ being a substitute for the punishment that humanity should have had to suffer.

The insight behind this theory is that Jesus Christ did something for us on the cross that we could not do on our own; something that is necessary for our salvation ("Christ died for us.")

But the obvious flaw in this theory is that it portrays God's motivation as something other than love.

Also, it strongly implies that there are almost two gods at work: a mean Father and a loving Son. And so, when pushed to its logical conclusions, it violates the basic tenet of unity in the Trinity. The moral influence theory was a corrective to the substitutionary atonement theory.

REFLECTION QUESTIONS

In what ways can a person be "at war" with God, or an enemy of God?

What do you think "the wrath" is in Romans 5:9? (In the original language, verse 9 does not contain "of God," which was added by translators.)

1. The wrath is God's eternal torment and punishment of sinners at the end of time.
2. The wrath is the negative consequences of our bad decisions that God does not prevent from happening to us.
3. The wrath is our eternal non-existence that will happen as a result of our lack of faith in God while we were alive.
4. The wrath is the guilt we experience.

When is it impossible for us to handle the responsibilities and consequences of our mistakes?

When in our lives are we not able to be independent and we need someone to be our substitute? How might these experiences help us understand the role Jesus plays in Romans 5:6-8?

In Romans 5:6, who takes the initiative to reconcile God and humanity?

What does it mean to be reconciled to God?

How do you deal with guilt?

How does the cross free us from guilt? How might it be misunderstood in such a way that increases our shame?

When you have a conflict with someone do you:
___ avoid them
___ attack them
___ look for their faults
___ line up allies
___ question yourself

What divides Christians?

How is the cross the "great equalizer" among people?

WHAT WE BELIEVE:

- On the cross, Christ did something that saves us from sin that we could not do for ourselves.
- The cross is a once and for all sacrifice that does not need to be repeated.
- The death of Christ alleviates human guilt.
- All persons are equal in light of the cross.
- Sin distorts, but does not eliminate, the image of God in humans. Salvation is a restoration of the image of God.

WHAT WE REJECT:

- The cross is a symbol of divine approval of child

abuse.
- The cross is a sacrifice that we must imitate.

MEDITATION EXERCISE:
"PRAYER OF CONFESSION"

Step 1: Read or sing the first stanza from "And Can It Be":
And can it be that I should gain
an interest in the Savior's blood!
Died he for me? Who caused his pain!
For me? Who him to death pursued?
Amazing love! How can it be
that thou, my God, shouldst die for me?
Amazing love! How can it be
that thou, my God, shouldst die for me?

Step 2: Pray: "God, forgive me for my sins and free me from my guilt." Name all those things that have separated you from God.

Step 3: Visualize Jesus, with his wounds, taking you in his arms and hugging you. When you look in his face, see his tears and his smile as he holds you. Hear him say to you, "All is well."

Step 4: Read or sing the following refrain from "And Can It Be":
'Tis mercy all, immense and free,
for O my God, it found out me!
'Tis mercy all, immense and free,
for O my God, it found out me!

4. A Dying Life: The Cross as Participation

GETTING STARTED

Which museum have you visited that does the best job of bringing history to life?

INTRODUCTION

Over the centuries, spiritual writers and mystics have seen the cross as something more than an historical event that happened to Jesus. For them, the crucifixion is a step in our spiritual process that culminates in transformation, blessing, and union with God.

Thomas a'Kempis wrote in "The Imitation of Christ": "Everything is founded on the cross and everything depends on our dying on the cross. There is no other way to life and interior peace except the holy way of the cross and our daily dying to self."[4]

This participatory view of the cross is one of the meanings of baptism. Just as the believer is immersed in the baptismal waters, so our faith undergoes a death and resurrection in the Spirit.

> ## Beyond Theories: Participation
>
> Before there were theories about the atonement, there was the experience of early believers. For them, the crucifixion was the spiritual process through which we enter into the unity of God — "become participants of the divine nature." (2 Peter 1:7) This unity with God entails victory over the forces of sin and death in one's self.
>
> What makes it possible for the crucifixion to be personal for us is the nature of Jesus Christ. For these early believers, Jesus is God who retraces and recovers the human experience through his earthly life. This is called "recapitulation." In Christ, God runs the gamut of the human experience, including death, in order to lead us through it and into the life of God.
>
> From this perspective the cross was often portrayed as the Tree of Life. Throughout history there are images of the cross sprouting leaves and bearing fruit. It plays on the irony of the cross as the life-nurturing atonement. This is in contrast to a legal perspective of the cross that one finds in the substitutionary theory.

If the solution that the cross offers is a participation in the death of Christ, what then is the problem? Sin is domination. It is something that controls us — possesses us — making us think and do those things that destroy us. The cross as the process of liberation in this session is the same theme in session one, but on a personal level.

READING

Romans 6:1-14

[1] What then are we to say? Should we continue in sin in order that grace may abound? [2] By no means! How can we who died to sin go on living in it? [3] Do you not know that all of us who have been baptized into Christ Jesus were baptized into his death? [4] Therefore we have been buried with him by baptism into death, so that, just as Christ was raised from the dead by the glory of the Father, so we too might walk in newness of life.

[5] For if we have been united with him in a death like his, we will certainly be united with him in a resurrection like his. [6] We know that our old self was crucified with him so that the body of sin might be destroyed, and we might no longer be enslaved to sin. [7] For whoever has died is freed from sin. [8] But if we have died with Christ, we believe that we will also live with him. [9] We know that Christ, being raised from the dead, will never die again; death no longer has dominion over him. [10] The death he died, he died to sin, once for all; but the life he lives, he lives to God. [11] So you also must consider yourselves dead to sin and alive to God in Christ Jesus.

[12] Therefore, do not let sin exercise dominion in your mortal bodies, to make you obey their passions. [13] No longer present your members to sin as instruments of wickedness, but present yourselves to God as those who have been brought from death to life, and present your members to God as instruments of righteousness. [14] For sin will have no dominion over you, since you are not under law but under grace.

REFLECTION QUESTIONS

Think of a persistent bad habit you have. When have you tried to break it, and what did you do?

What sorts of things can have "dominion" over a person?

What is the relationship between the crucifixion and resurrection in this passage?

What would our faith experience be if there was only the challenge to die with Christ without the hope of being raised with Christ?

Or, what would our faith experience be if there was only the goal of being raised with Christ without first dying with Christ?

How does the idea of "dying with Christ" run counter to our culture of pleasure and fulfillment?

Is there a difference between dying to self and dying to sin (v. 2)?

What's the difference between the weightlifter's slogan, "No pain, no gain" and Paul's statement, "If we have been united with him in a death like his, we will certainly be united with him in a resurrection like his."?

How might Romans 6 be misread and misused to deepen shame and self-injury?

WHAT WE BELIEVE:

- The crucifixion is an historical event that has meaning for us today.
- The Holy Spirit as the third "person" of the Trinity makes the cross meaningful for us.

WHAT WE REJECT:

The symbol of the cross promotes self-flagellation.

MEDITATION EXERCISE: "SIGN OF THE CROSS"

At the beginning of the day:

Step 1: At the beginning of your day, use water to remember that you have been baptized. For example, splash water in your face, run water over your hands, or stand beside a creek bed and listen to the water flowing.

Step 2: Recite Romans 6:3: "Do you not know that all of us who have been baptized into Christ Jesus were baptized into his death?"

Step 3: Think of one habit, thought, or attitude that you need to surrender to God to be free from its control (i.e. that you need to "die" to).

Throughout the day:

Option 1: Carry a small cross with you and periodically

feel it as a reminder of what you need to surrender to God that day. Repeat to yourself this one sentence prayer: "Surrender."

Option 2: Make the sign of the cross throughout the day as a reminder of what you need to surrender to God that day.

Repeat to yourself this one sentence prayer: "Surrender." (Making the sign of the cross: Using your right hand, you should touch your forehead at the mention of the Father; the lower middle of your chest at the mention of the Son; and the left shoulder on the word "Holy" and the right shoulder on the word "Spirit.")

At the end of the day:

Step 1: Like this morning, use water as a symbolic reminder of your baptism.

Step 2: Recite Romans 6:5, "For if we have been united with him in a death like his, we will certainly be united with him in a resurrection like his."

Step 3: Hold your palms upward and imagine receiving the new life and blessing that replaces what you have been surrendering throughout the day.

Step 4: Read or sing the following stanzas from "I Surrender All":
All to Jesus I surrender;
Lord, I give myself to thee;
fill me with thy love and power;
let thy blessing fall on me.

I surrender all, I surrender all,
all to thee, my blessed Savior,
I surrender all.

All to Jesus I surrender;
now I feel the sacred flame.
O the joy of full salvation!
Glory, glory, to his name!
I surrender all, I surrender all,
all to thee, my blessed Savior,
I surrender all.

5. A Necessary Obedience: The Cross as Obedience

GETTING STARTED

Have you ever been misunderstood or criticized for doing the right thing?

INTRODUCTION

The cross has been an inspiration for prophets of the 20th century.

Martin Luther King, Jr. often talked about his commitment to nonviolent dissent as the cross.

Archbishop Oscar Romero saw the cross in his work for peace in El Salvador.

During World War II, Dietrich Bonhoeffer found meaning for his resistance to the Third Reich by meditating on the cross.

In "The Cost of Discipleship" he wrote: "To endure the cross is not a tragedy; it is the suffering which is the fruit of an exclusive allegiance to Jesus Christ. When it comes, it is not an accident, but a necessity...If our Christianity has ceased to be serious about discipleship, if we have watered down the gospel into emotional uplift which makes no costly demands and which fails to distinguish between natural and Christian existence, then we cannot help regarding the cross as an ordinary, everyday calamity, as one of the trials and tribulations of life...The cross means sharing the suffering of Christ to the last and the fullest...When Christ calls a man, he bids him come and die."[5]

If the cross is the supreme symbol of obedience, what then is the problem? The cross saves us from the sin of selfishness. It challenges apathy and inspires commitment.

The cross as a symbol of obedience is the culmination of the four dimensions, which we previously discussed. The obedience it inspires is not a doomed endeavor because of the victory over evil that it has achieved. It is a symbol we can relate to because it demonstrates Christ's affinity with us. Our obedience is possible because of the reconciliation and empowerment we have received through it.

This session is a meditation on the cross as our example and inspiration for discipleship.

READING

Mark 8:31-38

[31]Then he began to teach them that the Son of Man must undergo great suffering, and be rejected by the elders, the chief

priests, and the scribes, and be killed, and after three days rise again. ³²He said all this quite openly.

And Peter took him aside and began to rebuke him. ³³But turning and looking at his disciples, he rebuked Peter and said, 'Get behind me, Satan! For you are setting your mind not on divine things, but on human things.'

³⁴He called the crowd with his disciples, and said to them, 'If any want to become my followers, let them deny themselves and take up their cross and follow me. ³⁵For those who want to save their life will lose it, and those who lose their life for my sake, and for the sake of the gospel, will save it. ³⁶For what will it profit them to gain the whole world and forfeit their life? ³⁷Indeed, what can they give in return for their life? ³⁸Those who are ashamed of me and of my words in this adulterous and sinful generation, of them the Son of Man will also be ashamed when he comes in the glory of his Father with the holy angels.'

REFLECTION QUESTIONS

What was so tempting about Peter's advice for Jesus? How did it remind Jesus of his earlier temptations?

Which would be the hardest for you: the psychological suffering, the physical suffering, or the rejection by others?

Verse 34 describes a process of obedience: deny self, take up your cross, follow Christ. What do each one of these steps mean to you?

What kind of faith experience would you have if you:
- don't deny yourself but try to pick up your cross?
- don't pick up your cross but deny yourself?

How does Mark 8:35-6 compare with our culture of self-fulfillment?

What excuses do we make for not following v. 34?

Read the Bonhoeffer quote in the introduction. What insights do you learn from his statement?

Liberal Protestants and the Cross

In the 19th century, liberal theology developed (first in Germany and then in America). Liberalism rejected orthodox views of the cross.

The early liberals criticized substitutionary theory as too abstract and too callous in its portrayal of God. Yet, at the same time, they were opposed to secularization and a total rejection of belief in God.

Liberal theology developed as a middle way between orthodoxy and secularism. It did this by reinterpreting Christianity with contemporary beliefs, such as pragmatism and evolution. For liberal theology, the way to make the Gospel relevant is to emphasize Christianity as an ethical way of life.

Echoing the moral influence theory, liberals criticized substitutionary theory as an affront to the moral character of God. At the same time they also favored naturalistic views of the nature of Christ, and Jesus as a moral leader.

Thus, liberal theologians favored moral concepts of atonement.

The cross inspires obedience and imitation.

WHAT WE BELIEVE:

- Discipleship requires sacrificial commitment.
- Carrying one's cross is a voluntary and intentional act.

WHAT WE REJECT:

- We earn our salvation through our imitation of Christ's obedience.
- The cross legitimates relationships of subservience.

MEDITATION EXERCISE:
'DIRTY WORK, HOLY WORK'

Step 1: Select a task that you hate doing. Do that task for someone else.

Step 2: Before you do the task, recite these words (that are adapted from the Great Thanksgiving prayer for communion):
"In remembrance of
God's mighty acts in Jesus Christ,
I offer myself in praise and thanksgiving
as a holy and living sacrifice,
in union with Christ's offering for us."

Step 3: If it is a task that allows you to think about other things while you do it (e.g. washing the dishes), meditate on Jesus's words in Mark 8:34-35: "If any want to become my followers, let them deny themselves and take up their cross and follow me. ^{35}For those who want to save their life will lose it, and those who lose their life for my sake, and for the sake of the gospel, will save it."

Step 4: After you have completed the task, offer God a prayer of thanksgiving for the privilege of doing the task for that person.

[1] In James Cone's "The Cross and the Lynching Tree"

[2] Louisville: Westminster John Knox Press, p. 77

[3] "The Crucified God: The Cross of Christ as the Foundation and Criticism of Christian Theology." New York: HarperCollins, 1974.

[4] New York: Vintage Books, XII.3, p. 66.

[5] New York: Touchstone Book, 1995, p. 88-89.

About the Author

Darren Cushman Wood is the senior pastor of North United Methodist Church in Indianapolis, Indiana. He has served small and large, rural and urban United Methodist churches for over 30 years. He is a graduate of the University of Evansville and Union Theological Seminary.

He is the author of two books, hymns, and numerous articles. He is an adjunct professor of labor studies at Indiana University. He is married to Ginny and as of this writing they have three adult children and one grandchild.

The North Study Series

www.ingramcontent.com/pod-product-compliance
Lightning Source LLC
LaVergne TN
LVHW021626080426
835510LV00019B/2774